CARL SANDBURG
Voice of the People

A CREATIVE PEOPLE IN THE ARTS AND SCIENCES
BOOK

Carl Sandburg: Voice of the People

BY RUTH FRANCHERE
ILLUSTRATED BY VICTOR MAYS

ABOUT THE BOOK: The colorful details of Carl Sandburg's interesting and varied life make exciting reading. In this biography, memorable scenes in Sandburg's life abound, and the author has carefully selected those incidents which helped Sandburg develop as a poet, historian, novelist, and biographer. Young readers will enjoy this closer acquaintanceship with Carl Sandburg, who devoted a loving heart, an observing eye, and a poetic voice to singing the praises of America—the land and its people. This book is one of Garrard's CREATIVE PEOPLE IN THE ARTS AND SCIENCES, which tell the life stories of the truly creative geniuses of the world and provide hours of worthwhile pleasure reading.

Subject classification: Biography
Sub-classification: American Poets, Lincoln biographers, Reading

ABOUT THE AUTHOR: Ruth Franchere was, like Carl Sandburg, "born on the prairie." Her childhood was spent in Waterloo, Iowa, and she later attended the University of Iowa. After graduation, Mrs. Franchere and her husband moved to Carl Sandburg's home state of Illinois where they lived for nine years. Before embarking on her own writing career, Mrs. Franchere, as a teacher of English Composition, encouraged many young writers in her classes. She taught at several universities including Portland State in Oregon where her husband is the Dean of the Division of Arts and Letters. This is her first book for Garrard.

Reading Level: Grade 5	**Interest Level: Grades 4–7**
144 pages . . . 5¾ x 8¼	**Publisher's Price: $2.59**

SBN 8116-4505-3

Illustrated with photographs and line drawings; full-color jacket; reinforced bindings; index

GARRARD PUBLISHING COMPANY

CARL SANDBURG

VOICE OF THE PEOPLE

by Ruth Franchere

illustrated by Victor Mays

GARRARD PUBLISHING COMPANY
Champaign, Illinois

To my sister Evelyn

who remembers Chicago

The author and publisher are grateful to Miss Margaret
Sandburg for the memories and other material which she
contributed, and for her assistance in checking the accuracy
of this manuscript about her father.

Selections on pages 97 and 98 from *Chicago Poems* by Carl Sandburg. Copyright 1916 by Holt, Rinehart and Winston, Inc. Copyright 1944 by Carl Sandburg. Reprinted by permission of Holt, Rinehart and Winston, Inc.

Excerpt on page 105 from "Prairie" from *Cornhuskers* by Carl Sandburg. Copyright 1918 by Holt, Rinehart and Winston, Inc. Copyright 1946 by Carl Sandburg. Reprinted by permission of Holt, Rinehart and Winston, Inc.

The following by permission of the publishers, Harcourt, Brace & World, Inc.: Excerpts on pages 110, 130 and 133, respectively, from *Rootabaga Stories; The People, Yes;* and *Abraham Lincoln: The War Years* by Carl Sandburg, published by Harcourt, Brace & World, Inc.

Picture credits:

Chicago Historical Society: p. 96

Haas, Joseph and Gene Lovitz, *Carl Sandburg: A Pictorial Biography* (Putnam). Photographs now in Gene Lovitz Carl Sandburg Collection, Knox College, Galesburg, Illinois: p. 41, 115

Frederic B. Knoop: p. 139 (top)

Knox College Archives: p. 71

Leviton-Atlanta from Black Star: p. 2

Dan J. McCoy from Black Star: p. 137, 140

Carl Sandburg Association: p. 9, 44, 68, 76, 78, 92

Dana Steichen: p. 121, 123

Edward Steichen: p. 82, 108, 124, 125, 127

Edward Steichen. Courtesy of Chicago Historical Society: p. 113

John Vachon, ©*Look Magazine:* p. 132

Wide World: p. 131, 135, 139 (bottom)

J
928
S

Standard Book Number: 8116-4505-3

Library of Congress Catalog Card Number: 79-87312

Contents

1. Life on Berrien Street

One day in the 1880's, when he was about seven years old, Carl August Sandberg decided to change his name to Charles.

"Call me Charlie," he told his older sister, Mary, and his younger brother, Martin. "All the boys I know have Swedish names like Carl. Charlie sounds more American."

Mary thought for a while. "I like Charlie, too," she said. And Martin agreed.

Soon afterward, the three decided to change their last name from Sandberg to Sandburg, because they thought the "u" was also more American. Before long their mother began to use the new spelling, too.

Since both of Charlie's parents had come from Sweden, they found English words hard to pronounce. His father called him Sholly. His mother and some of his playmates from other Swedish homes called him Sharlie. But he didn't care. He liked to sign his name Charles August Sandburg, and did so at school.

The Sandburgs were poor. When he was very young, August Sandburg, Charlie's father, had come to America as did many other Swedes who hoped for a better life. Some of them settled in Galesburg, a prairie town of about 10,000 people in western Illinois.

Mr. Sandburg worked hard for the Chicago, Burlington and Quincy Railroad, which was nicknamed the "Q." For ten hours a day, six days a week, he stood over the hot fire of a blacksmith's forge, heating, pounding, and shaping iron. He never earned more than fourteen cents an hour and never had a vacation, but Charlie did not once hear him complain. Mr. Sandburg was glad to have work.

Sometimes he would bang his hard calloused

Charlie's parents—Clara and August Sandburg

hand on the supper table and talk to his family about America. He spoke partly in Swedish, partly in English. "America is the best country in the world. America is freedom. A man can work hard and not starve. He can vote. He can send his children to school. They can learn to write."

Charlie knew how important that was to his father. Although Mr. Sandburg could read Swedish, he had never learned to write. He signed his name with an x.

August Sandburg worried about providing for his family. He needed more than his wages from the Q shop. In 1882, when Carl (later Charlie) was four years old, his father arranged to buy a house on East Berrien Street and gradually paid for it by taking in renters.

The house had ten rooms besides a long attic room on the third floor and four rooms in the basement. It was on a large lot with maple trees in front and space for a big garden in back.

He moved his wife, Clara, and the three children into the west side of the house. He rented the east side to two different families, and for several years housed a bachelor in the two other rooms.

After his long days at the forge, he made all the repairs on the house and worked in his garden until dark. He was proud of that house. Never in Sweden could he have bought such a place.

Charlie always remembered the evenings at home when he was very young. "Read to us, Papa," he begged as soon as chores were done.

Then Mr. Sandburg sat down at the kitchen table, turned up the lamp, and opened the only book in the house, the Bible he had brought with him from Sweden. The family gathered around to listen.

Charlie didn't understand all the Swedish words, but he liked to hear them. They sounded like music. Afterward, August Sandburg sometimes picked up his small accordion and played the one Swedish tune that he knew. Charlie never grew tired of the simple melody.

Clara Sandburg, Charlie's mother, usually sat near the lamp beside a large mound of clothes that she patched and mended. Although she was better educated than her husband, she seldom had time to read.

Charlie liked to watch the light flicker on his mother's straw-colored hair and see the sweet smile on her face when she looked up at her fine family. She did not worry the way her dark-haired, solemn husband did. She, too, worked from morning till night, but she could always manage to smile.

All the children had their chores to do as soon as they were old enough. A new baby, Emil, arrived when Charlie was seven, and three years later Esther was born. By this time, Charlie could do many of the household chores.

"More kindling, Sharlie," his mother called, and he would go into the cellar to split wood.

"*Friskt vatten*, Sholly," his father said whenever he wanted fresh water to drink. Then Charlie would take the pail out to the backyard and pump water from the well.

One of the hardest jobs, especially during the cold winters, was filling the washtubs every Monday morning with many buckets of rain water from the tank outside. But the job that he really hated came on winter days when his mother said, "Sharlie, the coal is gone."

Charlie would groan, pick up the coal hod, and open the back door. The only way he could make the job bearable was to think up wild stories about what he was doing.

As he stepped out into the snow, he told himself, "I'm an explorer going through a terrible blizzard." As he shoveled snow away from the coalbin door under the back porch, he muttered, "I must find shelter or I'll freeze to death."

Inside the coalbin, he pretended to be a miner. One day he even fastened a small tin can to his cap and pretended that it was a miner's lamp. When he swung a hammer to break up the large pieces of coal, he imagined that he was the poor "breaker boy" he had read about in a magazine, the *Youth's Companion*, that he borrowed from a friend. That breaker boy had worked all day in the coal mines. Charlie coughed and swayed as he worked, and the job seemed to go faster.

Life was not all work. Martin, called Mart, a year and a half younger, was his constant companion. Fair like his mother, with her cheerful disposition, Mart was quick to laugh.

By squeezing through a gap over the door, Charlie and Mart often raided the apple barrel, which was kept in a locked closet under the stairs. On hot days they went swimming with other neighborhood boys in a swimming hole at the edge of town.

But best of all, Charlie liked to play baseball.

"I've got the bat!" he would call from the center of the street as he brandished an old broom handle. "Where's the ball?"

"Here!" Mart would answer, holding up the five-cent rubber ball that they had wrapped round and round with string.

A shout came from one neighboring yard, then another. Someone placed one brick for home plate and another for first base. Tin cans made fine markers for second and third bases. A man's glove stuffed with cotton took the sting out of a fast ball.

The cry went up: "Play ball!"

Bare feet pounded on the dirt street. Nothing mattered but baseball until mothers called the boys to supper.

Berrien Street was a wonderful place when Charlie was young.

2. Books and Music

One day August Sandburg trudged home from the blacksmith shop carrying a mysterious package. Charlie met him at the gate.

"What is it, Papa?" he asked.

His father only smiled and walked around the house.

On the back porch, Charlie quickly filled the washbasin with warm water for his father. Washing up came before anything else, he knew.

"Mama! Mary! Everybody come! Papa has brought something home," Charlie called.

Still the father said nothing. He placed the big, heavy package in its brown paper on a high shelf and began to clean the day's grime from his hands. One ... two ... three times he emptied dirty water from the washbasin. Then he got out his pocketknife and slowly scraped the black lines from the cracks in his calloused hands.

All the children gathered around their mother, waiting, their eyes on the big package on the shelf. Only at Christmas did their father bring presents — an orange or a pocketknife or some other small gift for each child. Never before had he brought anything so big.

"Please hurry, Papa," Charlie whispered.

"Hush," his mother said. "Do you want your papa to unwrap his package with dirty hands?"

At last Mr. Sandburg was ready. He carried the package into the parlor and carefully laid it on the new marble-top table. Slowly he took off the brown paper wrapping.

"Oh-h-h!" everybody exclaimed.

"A book!" Charlie cried. "A big book!" He stepped forward and ran his fingers over the scrolls and figures on the black cover. He traced the shiny gilt letters. "Holy Bible," he whispered.

His mother opened the cover. Inside was a page for the names of the family. "I shall write all your names here," she said. "It is beautiful, August. Now all the children can read it."

Suddenly her face flushed and she clapped her hands to her cheeks. "How much did you pay?" she exclaimed.

"Six dollars and fifty cents," her husband answered proudly.

Everyone in the room gasped. That was a whole week's wages!

Slowly, reverently, Charlie turned the pages. Behind him he heard his father explain, "The little ones cannot understand Swedish. In America, they must learn to read the English Bible."

The new Bible remained in its place of honor on the parlor table. Almost every day Charlie went into the parlor and proudly turned the pages and read some of it. Nobody else he knew owned such a book — or any book at all.

Charlie read more than anyone else in the family, but the books belonged to the public library and had to be returned. Someday, he decided, he would buy many books and have bookcases to keep them in.

His mother must have had something like the same idea, only not so grand. One day when a salesman came to the door, she bought another book, *Cyclopedia of Important Facts of the World*. Mr. Sandburg grumbled about the 75¢ that she had spent.

But for Charlie, to own another book was wonderful. He read it over and over and memorized all the facts that he could cram into his head.

Shortly afterward his mother bought *A History of the World and Its Great Events*. It was three times the size of the first book. She paid $1.50 for it.

August Sandburg ranted and raved for a long time about her extravagance. He worked a whole day to earn that money.

"A Bible is important," he said. "A book about history is a foolish waste."

But it was not wasted on his son Charlie. "Mart," he said to his brother one day, "you like woodworking. Why don't you build us a bookcase for our library?"

"Our library!" Martin exclaimed. "Those two books? Besides I don't have the right tools."

"You can build it when you take manual training. We can save our old schoolbooks. And I can get some men to give me Duke cigarette coupons. I can get books about the Civil War with them."

Martin agreed to make the bookcase. Meanwhile Charlie collected coupons, sent for the books, and read all of them. But best of all he liked *A History of the World and Its Great Events*. From that book he learned to enjoy reading about people and events of other times.

It was a lucky day when Charlie entered the sixth grade where little Miss Lottie Goldquist was the teacher. She was part Swedish and full of energy. She took her students on field trips, taught them the names of flowers, and showed them how to break up rocks and look for leaf prints and other fossils. Charlie began to appreciate the beauty of the Illinois prairie.

"You can never get enough education," Miss Goldquist kept telling the class. When she found that Charlie Sandburg liked to read, she was delighted. She loaned him many books.

"Books are good friends," she told her pupils. She wanted the other students to read more, too.

Charlie read many more books about famous men of history, among them *Napoleon and his Marshals* and *Washington and his Generals*.

Miss Goldquist enjoyed poetry, and Charlie found that it appealed to him, too. It was like music. He memorized some of his teacher's favorite poems and often recited them to himself.

> Tell me not, in mournful numbers,
> Life is but an empty dream!

he would chant. The words called for music to go with them.

Papa played his accordion, and Mama hummed while she worked. Mary was learning to play chords on the little parlor organ.

Charlie wanted to make music of his own. He

carved a willow whistle and hummed through a comb covered with thin paper. He bought a tin fife and a ten-cent kazoo, a one-string instrument to hum into. Later he bought an ocarina, an oval toy with a mouthpiece and finger holes, that gave off different soft tones.

He even tried to make a banjo out of a cigar box by cutting a hole in it and stringing wires over it. But he couldn't get it to work.

One day he made a new friend, Willis Calkins. Willis had a fine voice and his father and mother could sing, too. Best of all, Willis could play the banjo!

"Is it hard to play?" Charlie asked one evening while he sat on the Calkins's porch and listened to "Sweet Polly Perkins on Arlington Green."

"Naw," Willis answered. "It's easy. You try."

He put the banjo into Charlie's hands and showed him how to make the chords and accompany the songs.

Charlie caught on at once. He was so excited that he knew he must have a banjo.

He had been working every morning before school sweeping out an office and emptying the spittoons for 25¢ a week. He had saved more than $2.

The next morning he raced down to a pawn shop on Main Street and found a banjo that he could buy for $2. He learned more chords from Willis while he earned a little more money. Then he took three lessons from a lady for 25¢ each.

From that time on, the banjo was an important accompaniment for the songs and poems that he learned.

3. The Terrible Debt

One February evening in 1889 when August Sandburg came home, his wife handed him a letter. He pulled out an official-looking piece of paper, stared at it, and shook his head.

"Come eat your supper," Clara Sandburg said kindly, knowing that he could not understand it. "Then we will read it together."

After supper Charlie and the other children were very quiet while their parents sat close to the lamp. Mrs. Sandburg read the strange words, slowly, to her husband. Neither of them could understand what they meant.

The next day, instead of putting on his work

clothes, Mr. Sandburg put on his black Sunday suit, white shirt, and black bow tie. After he left, Mrs. Sandburg told the children, "Papa is going to see a lawyer. He has a terrible worry."

The worry, they learned that night, was over a town lot their father had proudly bought five years before. From his small wages he had saved nickels, dimes, and quarters, week after week, for it. But the lawyer told him that a former owner had borrowed money on that land many years before. The debt, called a mortgage, had never been paid.

There was a trial. The judge said that August Sandburg had to pay the money—$804.24.

When he walked into the house that day, head down, all he could say was, *"Gud bavara!"* The three oldest children knew those words—"God help me!"

Although he was only eleven, Charlie understood what the terrible debt meant. His father could never pay it with his small wages.

"I'll help, Papa," Charlie said. "I'll look for more work after school. In two years, when I finish the eighth grade, I can leave school and get a full-time job."

Mary, who was three years older, had already started high school. The family decided that she should finish so that she could teach in a country school and help out. Country schools paid $30 a month.

Besides cleaning the real estate office every morning, Charlie soon began carrying papers for the Galesburg *Republican-Register*. Directly after school he went to the newspaper office. He took his papers from the press to a big table where he folded and counted them — one for each customer and one for himself.

From the beginning, Charlie was fascinated by the workings of the newspaper office. A reporter who went about town gathering news and writing it in a notebook seemed a very important person to him. Each day Charlie saw the reporter take his stories to another man called a typesetter. He watched the typesetter pick out letters from a box in front of him and set them into a frame just the width of a newspaper column. Later the words the reporter had written in his notebook would be in the newspapers that Charlie carried from house to house.

For more than two years, he carried fifty or sixty papers six days a week. His route was two miles long. He took pride in throwing his papers just so and having them land smack against the door.

Snow and rain often made his work hard, but he was glad to take home the silver dollar that he earned each week. He was glad to have his own copy of the paper to read, too.

During Charlie's last year of school the baby, Freddy, was born. The family of eight needed more money, so Charlie looked for more work.

"I'm going to carry Chicago papers, too," he announced one evening. "I'll get seventy-five cents a week and extra money on Sundays."

Each Sunday, six different Chicago papers came in early on the fast mail train. Charlie started out at seven-thirty pulling a small wagon loaded with papers. He finished at one o'clock, richer by at least fifty cents.

Then he allowed himself his one extravagance. Five or six of the hungry carrier boys went into a little lunchroom.

"One and a bun," Charlie ordered. "Me, too," the next boy said. Every week they all ordered the same thing, a fried egg in a bun. They ate and laughed and talked. They felt good about their day's business.

With other odd jobs — spading gardens, picking pails of potato bugs, and cleaning old bricks — Charlie made about twelve dollars a month. Most of that he took home to his father.

When Charlie finished the eighth grade, he knew that his school days were over. But there was no time to feel sorry for himself. He would just have to read and study on his own, he decided.

He got a full-time job delivering milk for a man named Burton. At five-thirty each morning his mother came up to the attic room where he slept with Mart and shook him gently.

"Get up, Sharlie," she whispered. "It's time."

Charlie rolled out of bed, picked up his clothes,

and stumbled down the stairs. As he dressed in the warm kitchen, his mother put a hearty breakfast on the table. He was doing a man's work and needed a man's meal.

To save the five-cent carfare Charlie walked two miles, sometimes in snow or rain, to Mr. Burton's barn. Seven days a week he loaded big cans of milk into the wagon. Then he drove from house to house and delivered the milk, pouring it into crocks or pitchers.

One October day when he woke up, his throat felt tight and very sore. He couldn't even swallow his breakfast.

"You go back to bed," his mother said. "Mart can go and tell Mr. Burton that you're sick."

Charlie worried for two days about losing his job. Then he forced himself to go back to work, even though he was still weak and unable to eat.

In a few days Mart, too, was sick. And then the two small boys, Emil, age seven, and Freddy, age two, had the same illness and could not swallow their food.

The family moved a narrow cot down to the kitchen, the only warm room in the house. They put the small boys on it and watched over them, but they did not get better. Finally Mr. Sandburg said, "Sholly, get the doctor."

When he arrived, the doctor looked into the children's throats, shook his head sadly, and spoke the dreaded word, "diphtheria." There was nothing he could do for them. Three days later, little Freddy stopped breathing. In half an hour, Emil, too, was gone.

The tragedy was doubly hard on all the family. Besides the terrible sorrow over the loss of the beloved children, there were more bills for the doctor and the funeral.

All that cold winter Charlie worked on the milk wagon. He had no money for warm boots. To keep his feet from freezing, he ran to the grocery store, stopped by the stove for a few minutes, and then ran the rest of the way to Mr. Burton's barn. If he was late, Mr. Burton grumbled. Finally Charlie quit and got a job as general helper in a drugstore.

That same year, 1893, many banks and businesses failed throughout the United States. Even the railroads made very little money.

August Sandburg and the other workers at the Q yards talked about the depression, but none of them understood what had brought it on. Fear crept over all of them as, one by one, the men lost their jobs.

One day Mr. Sandburg's boss said to him, "You're a fine worker, August, but I'll have to cut your work to four hours a day. You'll get about sixteen dollars a month."

Instead of butter, the family now spread lard on their bread and sprinkled it with salt. They ate potatoes from their garden, and they used the cheapest coal for the kitchen stove.

When Mary graduated from high school, Charlie somehow saved a few dollars so that she could have a white dress for the ceremony.

During Mary's school years, Charlie had read all of her textbooks. He also borrowed books from the public library, including one called *How To Educate Yourself*.

But no matter how much he read, there was often a hollow feeling inside him. He was only a druggist's helper. With a high school education he could do something important or interesting. At least he could teach in a country school, even though the idea did not especially interest him.

As Charlie swept out the drugstore, opened boxes, and ran errands, he often remembered the excitement of his first visit to the *Republican-Register* office. A newspaper reporter could have a rewarding life, he knew. But only a man with an education could be a reporter.

What was the good of a brain if a person wasn't allowed to use it? he asked himself. There was no answer for him in Galesburg.

4. Growing Up in a Hurry

Even though he was always looking for extra jobs, Charlie found time for fun, too. The game he enjoyed the most was baseball. A group he played with regularly seemed very good to him.

Charlie followed the baseball news every day and knew the names of all the leading players in the big leagues. He became such a fan that he even dreamed about baseball. When he was sixteen, the idea of becoming a professional ball player started to grow in his mind. Professional baseball might be the important career he was looking for, he thought.

One day Skinny Seeley showed up with a Spalding big-league regulation ball. Charlie

couldn't believe his eyes. He took the ball in his hand and smacked it into his old glove to hear the sound of it.

"Where'd you get it?" he asked in awe.

"Bought it myself," Skinny answered. "Dollar and a half!"

"Dollar and a half!" Charlie exclaimed.

Soon afterward Charlie managed to buy a secondhand big-league fielder's glove. With the new ball and glove, he and Skinny often practiced batting and catching flies in a nearby pasture. Before long, Charlie believed he was almost ready for a minor league.

One afternoon at practice, his head buzzing with plans, he banged his fist into his big glove and shouted, "Let her fly!"

Skinny hit a long, high ball. Charlie ran for it, making believe that he was catching for a minor league. A brilliant catch was almost within his grasp when, suddenly, his right foot slammed into a hole, and he crashed to the ground.

He lay stunned for a moment. Then slowly he sat up and stared at his foot. Blood oozed through a big gash in his shoe. In the hole in the ground he saw the jagged edge of a broken bottle.

"Yeow!" he yelled as he pushed himself up. "My foot! My foot!" he cried as he limped toward Doctor Taggard's house a block away, while Skinny supported him.

The doctor came out the door as Charlie hobbled up the steps. "Sit down, boy," he said quietly. "Take off your shoe and sock. Slowly, now. I'll get my bag."

The calm words of the doctor quieted Charlie. He gritted his teeth while he pulled off the slashed shoe and the ragged sock. He tensed his lips as the doctor took out bits of glass and dirt, poured some stinging liquid into the gash, and sewed it together with a long, curved needle. Charlie even tried to laugh and pretend it was nothing.

Back home, his mother comforted him. But while his foot mended, Charlie realized that something had happened to his secret dream of baseball fame. It was only a dream, after all. He wasn't really good enough.

There was a big empty place in his life again. Galesburg seemed very small, and he wanted to get away. But how? He had only eight dimes put away in a little bank.

"Papa," he said one evening, "a railroad worker can have a free pass to go anywhere, can't he?"

His father nodded. "But I don't want to go," he said.

"I've heard you can get a pass for any member of the family," Charlie persisted. "Get one for me *please*, Papa. I want to go to Peoria, to the State Fair. I've never been on a train."

Mrs. Sandburg listened and nodded. "That's right, August," she said. "A railroad man's oldest boy should ride on a train once."

And so it was decided. Charlie got his pass. With a lunch in one pocket and his eight dimes in the other, he set out alone for Peoria, Illinois, fifty miles away. There he stepped off the train into a big town crowded with people.

Like a traveler seeing the world for the first time, he walked up and down the streets looking into store windows and admiring the big buildings. Then he went out to the fairground and walked past all the exhibits of farm animals, machinery, and even ladies' needlework. He tried his luck at the shooting galleries, saw sideshows, and rode on the merry-go-round.

When his money was gone, he went back into town and sat for a long time just looking at the broad Illinois River. He watched the steamboats go by and wondered where they were going and how long it would take them to get there. Finally, he took a late train home.

For a while Charlie felt better about his life. Although he had been away for only one day, he had seen new things. His world was now larger than the boundaries of Galesburg.

With fresh determination, he made up his mind that he must learn a trade. He must get ahead somehow, now that he was sixteen.

"Why not try barbering?" someone suggested.

So he got a job as porter in the Union Hotel barber shop. He washed floors and windows, shined shoes, cleaned spittoons, and scrubbed

Charlie Sandburg was a porter in the Union
Hotel barber shop when this picture was taken.

the backs of men at the public baths next door. He earned three dollars a week and tips.

All fall and winter he worked in the barber shop. He listened when the customers talked and noted how some of them made a story interesting, but he didn't learn much about barbering. By spring he knew he had chosen the wrong trade.

Again he worked on a milk wagon. He walked all the way to the milkman's barn each morning and back home each night. His route took him through the Knox College campus and past the college's Old Main building. Here Abraham Lincoln and Stephen A. Douglas had held their famous debate 37 years before. He often stopped to read Lincoln's words inscribed on the bronze plate at the entrance of Old Main. "He is blowing out the moral lights around us, when he contends that whoever wants slaves has a right to hold them."

Those words gave Charlie a great deal to think about on his way to work. He was lucky not to be a slave, he thought. He could quit his job whenever he liked. Or could he? What would he do then?

After about a year and a half on the milk truck, Charlie asked for a raise and was turned down. So he decided again to look for something better.

No steady jobs were to be found. He was a tinsmith's helper for two days; then he washed bottles in a pop-bottling factory for two weeks. He was an ice cutter, and a stagehand at the auditorium. He tried everything.

There were many boys in Galesburg during those hard times who were also looking for work, but most of them did not seem to worry about the future and had fun whenever they could. So Charlie kept his worries to himself and had fun with them.

The boys gave each other nicknames like "Frenchy" or "Monk" or "Bohunk." Charlie's name became "Cully."

One Sunday afternoon, Charlie and his friends were sitting around Olsen's store when they decided to have their pictures taken. They counted and found they were a group of twelve.

The Dirty Dozen dressed in their Sunday best.
Charlie is at the far right in the top row.

"The Dirty Dozen!" someone said, and every-one laughed. From that day on the name stayed with them.

The Dirty Dozen played harmless pranks. They walked around the square on Saturday nights and bought themselves treats of cream puffs. They even got arrested one hot day for swimming without clothes in the old swimming hole on the edge of town.

That year a number of politicians lectured in Galesburg. Charlie and his friends went to hear most of them. On a platform down by the Q tracks they heard William Jennings Bryan, the Democratic Candidate for President. Later, on the Knox College campus they listened to Robert Ingersoll, a Peoria lawyer, argue against the Democrats. Although most of the Dirty Dozen did not understand all they heard, going to free lectures was something to do.

But Charlie listened and questioned and wanted to learn more. He began to read about politics in the Chicago papers. He read *The People's Party Campaign Book* and some of Bryan's speeches several times. Soon Bryan, a young liberal from Nebraska who wanted to improve conditions for the great masses of poor people, became Charlie's hero.

At home Charlie argued about politics every night. Although he could never influence his father, who was a Republican, he liked to argue. Mary thought Charlie should be a lawyer, but Charlie thought he'd be a better newspaperman.

About that time he made a new friend, John Sjodin. John's parents were Swedes who had moved to Galesburg from Chicago. There they had seen terrible poverty. Father and son had turned against a society in which there were extremely rich and extremely poor.

"We need a new kind of government," John told Charlie. "Working people must organize and get political power if they want to be better off."

"Are folks really worse off in Chicago than in Galesburg?" Charlie asked.

"Worse off! You ought to see 'em. No jobs. Begging in the streets," John answered. "But the rich—they've got everything. And they run everything in this country. You'll never really understand what's wrong with America unless you've seen city life for yourself. You've never been out of this little town."

"I've been to Peoria," Charlie objected.

"*Peoria*! You couldn't learn much there. You ought to go to Chicago."

Charlie shook his head. It was impossible. But then he began to think about it day and night.

5. Chicago!

Eighteen-year-old Charlie Sandburg sat on the wicker seat of a Q coach. His heart beat in time with the fast rhythmic click of the wheels as they carried him closer and closer to Chicago. In his hand was the pass he had wrung from his father after days of begging and arguing. In his pocket was $1.50—all that he could scrape together.

But he did not worry. His friend John Sjodin had told him how to get along on very little.

Suddenly the conductor pushed open the door and called, "Chicago!"

As the train screeched to a stop, Charlie peered out at the crush of people and wagons and handcarts. He moved to the front of the car and swung off the steps into the crowd — looking, listening, taking in everything.

First he headed for Pittsburgh Joe's, a place that John had told him about. He sat on a stool and devoured a big stack of pancakes with molasses and a cup of coffee — all for five cents.

Then, without wasting a minute, he started sightseeing. Up one street and down another he went. He listened to the clang of trolley cars and the clatter of horses' hoofs on the cobblestone streets. He stood under the elevated lines and watched the framework shake as the cars roared by overhead.

Dressed in his work clothes and old hat, the small-town boy wandered through all the big department stores on State Street and stared at the elegant displays of merchandise. He stood for a while in front of the Chicago *Daily News* and *Record* buildings. He wanted to go inside and tell someone that he had carried their papers,

but he didn't quite dare. Each night he went to a variety show where he could get a seat in the top gallery for ten cents.

Twice a day, he returned to Pittsburgh Joe's for a bowl of meat stew with bread and coffee for ten cents. At night, tired, happy, his head reeling with all he had seen and done, he went to a hotel on South State Street. For a quarter he had a bed with used sheets in a room where dust and refuse filled the corners.

On the last day, his third, he went into a saloon and helped himself to the free lunch at the counter.

"Small beer," he said to the barkeeper as he laid down his nickel.

He did not like beer, but he wanted to see the inside of one of the Chicago saloons that he had heard so much about.

His money was almost gone. For the last time, he walked down to the shore of Lake Michigan and looked at the great expanse of glittering water. Then he had to go home.

Back on Berrien Street he appreciated his

mother's good cooking and the clean room that he had slept in since he was four years old. But he missed the noise and the crowds. He wanted to go back to Chicago.

Only one event broke the monotony of the next months. On October 7, 1896, Knox College celebrated the 38th anniversary of the Lincoln-Douglas debates. Twenty thousand people came to the celebration.

Charlie pushed through the crowd to look at the men on the platform that had been set up next to the college. He was disappointed in the speeches, for they were dull.

But he had a chance to hear the president of the New York Central Railway, a man who had worked hard for Lincoln's election for President. He saw Robert Todd Lincoln, the great man's son, and wondered what he and his famous father had talked about. Charlie also heard the man who had gone to Chicago back in 1860 to nominate Lincoln for President. Civil War times came alive for him that day.

For a while, Charlie was cheered by the

realization that even great men like Lincoln were often discouraged and depressed. But by June of 1897, when he was nineteen years old, he knew that he was beginning to hate Galesburg. He still couldn't find a decent job or learn a trade. All his pals had their girl friends now, but he was shy with girls.

His talks with John Sjodin and his experiences in Galesburg and Chicago had made him eager to help the underprivileged people of the country. But he had no idea how to begin.

Even though he was sure his family would never understand, Charlie made up his mind that he must leave Galesburg again — go farther away and stay longer. He must see more of the world and find out what his place in it should be.

6. Hobo Trail

Charlie made all his plans to leave Galesburg before he told his family. He would not beg his father for another pass. This time he would get along without help from anyone. He was a full-grown man now — five feet ten inches tall.

He decided to take no luggage. He put on a black sateen shirt and his coat, vest, and trousers. Into each pocket he stuffed something he might need — a small bar of soap, needle and thread, comb, razor, a knife, two handkerchiefs. Last he put in all his money, $3.25.

He picked up his slouch hat and went down to the kitchen where his family sat around the table. It was noon, and his mother was dishing up the food.

He took his place at the table and tried not to look at her, but he could tell that she was looking at him and his clothes. When he glanced up he could see the tears in her eyes.

"You going away, Sharlie?" she asked.

He nodded. There was a lump in his throat.

"Where you going this time?"

"I don't know, Mama," he answered. "Kansas, maybe. I hear there's work in the wheat fields."

He finished his meal as quickly as he could. Then he stood up and kissed his mother good-bye. He waved his hand toward his father and the others at the table and hurried out. He could not bear to look back.

As he neared the station, he saw a freight train waiting. At a signal it began to pull out.

Suddenly all the discouragement of the past months dropped away. Charlie raced alongside and jumped into an open boxcar. On that bright

June afternoon he was free. He would see rivers and mountains, he told himself; he would meet new people. Each day would be a great adventure.

For several hours he stood in the open doorway and watched the long straight rows of new corn sweep by. They had never looked so beautiful. He read the names on the small stations along the way — names he had heard all his life.

At last the train came to a great river. It was the Mississippi! That big line on the map that divided the country was real water!

When the train stopped at Fort Madison, on the west side of the river, Charlie jumped off, ran to the riverbank, and stamped his feet on the rich Iowa earth. For the first time in his nineteen years, he had stepped out of Illinois!

From that moment on, Charlie put Illinois firmly behind him. The joy of pioneering carried him through good days and bad ones.

He did all kinds of work for a little money and food, but he never stayed anywhere for long. He unloaded kegs of nails from a Mississippi River steamboat. He worked with a railroad gang, threshed wheat, picked fruit, and washed dishes. He knocked on back doors and offered to chop wood for meals.

He rode in boxcars or on top of passenger cars. One night he could not find an empty boxcar, so he stood on the bumpers between two cars and held onto the brake rods. He was so tired he began to doze. Suddenly he awoke, heard the click of wheels under him, and knew what might have happened to him in another second. For a long hour he kept moving some part of his body — his head, a hand, or a foot — so that he would not fall asleep again. When the train stopped, he got off with a groan of relief and promised himself, "Never again!"

He slept in haylofts, in shacks, or under the stars. Usually he had only a few sheets of newspaper for a mattress, but he slept well.

He liked meeting the many kinds of people along the way. In hobo camps, in boxcars, beside railroad tracks, he joined professional bums who bragged about never doing a day's work in their lives. They called themselves "gaycats" and gave Charlie good advice about how to get along on the road.

They had a special language that he soon learned, too. A "lump" was a package of bread and meat handed out by a kind housewife. A "sitdown" was a meal offered at a kitchen table. A "shack" was a brakeman who would order him off a train if he didn't watch out.

At night around campfires near the tracks they told stories and jokes about their many

adventures and sang songs of the road. Charlie jotted these down in little notebooks so that he could repeat them for his family and friends at home. When it came his turn, he sang for the "gaycats" and wished he had brought his banjo.

Once in a while Charlie found a wanderer like himself who had to get away from home for a time.

"I like to sleep under the stars," one older man explained. "I learn a lot about life from studying the stars."

A farm boy from Indiana, about Charlie's age, said, "I'm heading for Alaska. How about coming with me? We'll get rich digging for gold."

Charlie was tempted, but he shook his head. "That's too far away," he answered.

From June to September Charlie moved slowly westward. One sunny morning, as he got off at a station, he saw great mountains reaching up into the sky.

"The Rocky Mountains!" he gasped.

Three months before, he had told himself he

would see rivers and mountains. Now he had seen the greatest of both!

The nights were growing cold. Charlie knew he had to make up his mind. Should he go on to the coast or back to Galesburg?

One day earlier in the summer, he had walked by an old bookstore. In the window was a battered book called *Cyclopedia of Useful Information*. The price was five cents. The book reminded him of home and the books his mother had bought for him so long ago. He bought it and read it when he was lonely.

Now, when he was trying to decide what to do, he felt that book in his pocket and realized he was growing homesick.

Still, he delayed making a decision. He went to Denver and spent two weeks there. He washed dishes in the best hotel and ate the best meals of his entire trip. Once in a while he stopped by an Army recruiting office and read the posters.

At last he decided he was ready to go home. From one train to another he made his way back east. To pass the time, he read his book and memorized many of the facts. On one page was a poem, said to be a favorite of Abraham Lincoln. He memorized that, too, and often said it to himself. It began:

Oh, why should the spirit of mortal be proud?
Like a swift fleeting meteor, a fast-flying cloud,
A flash of the lightning, a break of the wave,
He passes from life to his rest in the grave.

In Nebraska City, he stopped at a big brick house and chopped wood for two "sitdowns." The man of the family gave him his old wool suit. It was better than any suit Charlie had ever had. Now he could go home looking less like a bum.

Charlie's last night under the stars was filled with the sweet scent of ripe Illinois corn. On the afternoon of October 15, he walked into the house on Berrien Street.

"Sharlie!" his mother cried. "We thought you'd never come back."

"You look fine," Mary exclaimed. "You've got a new suit."

"Where have you been? Tell us everything," Mart insisted.

Charlie smiled and told them all the good things about his trip. He repeated some of the stories and sang some of his new songs. But only to Mart did he tell more, like the time when he fell asleep riding the bumpers of the fast-moving train.

Charlie moved back into the old life, first on a milk route and then as a painter's helper to learn the trade. But he knew the four months on the road had changed him, and he now had greater self-respect. He was a good storyteller, and he was not so shy, even with girls. His family and his friends knew he was different, too, but they could not say how.

The real difference was deep inside him, he decided. He now had hope. Once in a while he read his little notebooks. Perhaps someday, he thought, he could write about his experiences.

7. Soldier

Soon an unexpected event gave Charlie something new to think about. The United States battleship *Maine* was sunk in the harbor at Havana, Cuba. Newspapers accused the Spanish, who owned Cuba, of blowing it up. Men on the streets echoed the newspapers and called for war.

"Spain should give Cuba her independence, anyway," they said. "Let's fight to free the Cuban people."

Charlie suddenly remembered the Army posters he had read. If war were declared, he could enlist and see more of the world, he thought. He would have many experiences to tell and write about.

On April 25, 1898, President McKinley finally declared war, and on the following day Charlie was one of the first to sign up. Although he was only twenty, like many others he gave his age as twenty-one. He was sworn into Company C, Sixth Infantry Regiment of Illinois Volunteers.

Then he went home and told his family. They were troubled and sad, but they knew they could not stop him.

"We'll be proud to have a soldier in the family," Mart said, "but we don't want you to be killed."

Charlie hadn't thought about being killed.

"Aw, the war won't last long," he laughed. "I just hope it isn't over before I get to Cuba, though. Think of all the traveling I'll get to do."

The whole town went down to the Q station to see their boys off. Mothers and wives cried. Others cheered as the train slowly pulled out for Springfield, Illinois, the state capital.

During the ride, the boys joked and laughed. They made friends with the other volunteers

from farms and small towns near Galesburg. All felt like heroes.

But when the train reached Springfield, they began to learn what army life was really going to be like. They were marched out to the livestock building on the grounds of the State Fair and bedded down on the straw in the cow stalls. They did not feel like heroes any longer.

On a hot day in May they were issued leftover Civil War uniforms—heavy blue wool shirts, coats, and trousers meant for winter wear.

Later, they were moved to a camp seven miles from Washington, D.C. There they ate beans cooked with wormy pork which made them all sick. Through sweltering days, they drilled, marched, and stood guard two hours out of every six.

During the lonely guard duty, Charlie passed the time by reciting every poem he had ever learned. Across the field he could hear the rich baritone of a corporal singing the popular song, "Guess I'll Have to Telegraph My Baby." Charlie knew he, too, was cheering himself up.

Some things, however, made the Army seem worthwhile to Charlie. When he was stationed in Springfield, Illinois, he visited the state capital in his few hours off duty. He stood in front of Abraham Lincoln's first home and saw for himself that it was no better than the home of many a Swedish boy in Galesburg. In Washington he looked at the White House and thought about the long, lonely hours of the night when Lincoln had made his difficult decisions.

Company C was sent from Washington to Charleston, South Carolina, to await transport to Cuba. There Charlie got his first exciting glimpse of the Atlantic Ocean. He went swimming with the other boys from Illinois and filled his mouth with water.

"Hey!" he yelled. "It *does* taste like salt!"

Whenever he found time, he wrote his experiences in a diary and sent long letters to the Galesburg *Evening Mail*, to be published.

In Charleston, Company C was finally ordered to board the *Rita*. For six days the old freighter rolled toward Cuba and war.

Charlie and some of his buddies in Company C
Charlie is seen in the white circle.

At last they reached Guantanamo Bay, Cuba
and learned that the Spanish fleet had been
destroyed. The war there was over, but they
were to be sent to Puerto Rico.

"Where's Puerto Rico?" the soldiers asked.
"What are we going to do there?"

Charlie tried to remember his geography.
Puerto Rico was another Spanish island nearby,
he recalled. He could only guess that orders
had come to take that island, too.

A week later, the *Rita* steamed into a harbor

on the south coast of Puerto Rico. For no reason that anyone could figure, Company C began a nightmare march across the island and back again. Swarms of mosquitoes attacked them day and night. Drizzling rain kept their heavy wool uniforms constantly wet. Hardtack and "Red Horse," stringy canned beef that smelled so strong they could scarcely eat it, became the usual daily fare.

As they grew weaker, Charlie and the others discarded their 50 pounds of useless gear, piece by piece, beside the road.

At the end of each day one of the boys cried, "Shirts off! Inspection!"

Everyone pulled off his filthy shirt and hunted for ticks, called graybacks, and squashed them.

At last the long nightmare was over. They dragged themselves across the gangplank onto the *Rita*. They were going home!

Charlie weighed in at 130 pounds. During his four months in the army he had lost 22 pounds; his cheeks were hollow and his skin was yellow.

A month later, with his discharge paper and pay in his pocket, Charlie reached Galesburg. His mother exclaimed over his loss of weight. His father smiled at him as he had never smiled before.

"Here is my discharge paper, Papa," Charlie said. "You can have it."

August Sandburg held it in his hands for a long time. Then he handed it to his wife.

"A good soldier, service honest and faithful," she read aloud.

"We must have it framed to hang on the parlor wall," her husband said proudly.

After Charlie gave his father $50.00 of his Army pay, he had $53.73 left. It was the most money he had ever had at one time in his life.

"What are you going to do now?" Mart asked.

Charlie grinned. "Maybe I'll go to college," he answered.

"College!" Mart exploded. "Why, you didn't even go to high school."

"I know," Charlie said. "But one of the guys in Company C, who's been going to Lombard

College, says the reading I did should take its place. He thinks maybe I can get free tuition for a year at Lombard because of Army service."

In a few days the arrangements were made. Then a member of the Dirty Dozen got Charlie a part-time job in the fire department for ten dollars a month. The money would pay for books and clothes.

It was a proud day in the Sandburg household when the immigrant parents learned the news. Their oldest son would go to college!

Lombard College at the turn of the century

8. College

There were two well-known colleges in Galesburg. The larger one was Knox College. Lombard was only about one-third as large, with 125 students and 12 teachers.

Charlie was glad to be going to Lombard which had been founded as the Illinois Liberal Institute. He liked the idea of going to a liberal college.

Besides, he knew it very well. The campus was only a few blocks from home and, as a small boy, he had peeked into the classrooms. Later he and other barefoot boys had sneaked up to the little gallery over the chapel and listened to the Commencement Exercises. Charlie had watched with envy and awe as the graduates received their diplomas.

With free tuition, some Army pay, and his part-time job, Charlie had no worries. He bought books and supplies, a fireman's shirt and boots, and a bicycle. Then he enrolled in classes in Latin, English, inorganic chemistry, drama, and public speaking.

At night he slept on the second floor of the firehouse with fifteen other men. When the gong sounded he jumped up, pulled on his trousers and boots, and slid down the brass pole in the center of the room. In a flash he was up on the wagon seat, slapping the reins across the backs of two fast bays while the other firemen leaped onto the wagon. Then off they sped to the fire.

When the fire whistle blew during a class, he left quickly and telephoned the firehouse. If he was needed, he bicycled to the fire as fast as he could go.

It was a good job, he knew. He could study at home and get to the firehouse by ten o'clock.

Charlie worked hard and made good grades. In addition to his regular assignments he read many other books, for he knew he had to catch up with the students who had gone to high school.

One day near the end of his first year, as he was leaving the college, Charlie saw four officers from his old Army outfit waiting for him. He could tell they had exciting news.

One of the men explained at once. "We have the honor to tell you," he said, "that a man from Company C is to be appointed to West Point Military Academy. The officers chose you."

Charlie couldn't believe his ears. "You mean me? To West Point?" he exclaimed.

They all nodded.

"Of course you'd have to go to the Academy to take the examinations," a sergeant added. "They're pretty stiff. But you're always reading books, so you ought to pass. What do you say?"

Charlie grinned. "I don't know why you fellows chose me," he said. "That's quite an honor, all right. Sure I'd like to try. Thanks a lot!"

With high hopes Charlie went off to the Military Academy in New York State. There doctors examined him and found him physically fit.

Then he took the written examinations. In such subjects as literature and history he did very well, but in mathematics and the rules of grammar he found that the high school years he had missed left a gap in his knowledge. He failed the examinations.

Back home again Charlie enrolled at Lombard for a second year. But his tuition-free time was over, so he had to find other jobs besides the one he had at the firehouse. He never resented having to work, however, for to him, work was a normal way of life.

He got the job of bell-ringer for the college. At the end of classes he raced up the steps of the bell tower. He rang the bell, waited five minutes, and then rang it again for the next classes to start. He did not waste even those few minutes, for the bell tower was filled with old books

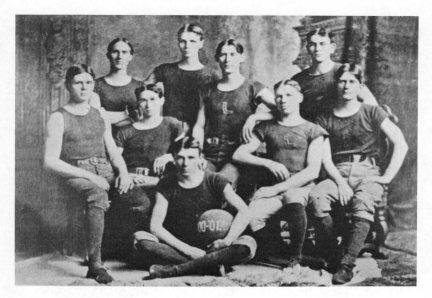

Charlie, holding the ball, was a member of the
1900-1901 basketball team of Lombard College.

discarded from the college library. No matter
what they were, he read them, because to him
all books were precious.

Later he had a job as janitor at the gymnasium.
He also went from door to door selling stereoscopic views — double pictures taken with a
special camera with two lenses side by side.
When the pictures were put into a viewer, they
had a three-dimensional effect.

Nearly every housewife had a viewer on her
parlor table and a small basket beside it filled

with views of such places as Niagara Falls and the Ruins of Pompeii. Charlie liked selling, because he could meet all kinds of people.

Jobs did not hinder Charlie from taking part in college activities, and soon he was one of the important men on the campus. He was business manager of the college newspaper, the *Lombard Review*, and wrote for it, too. Later he became editor-in-chief. He captained the basketball team, sang with the college glee club, joined a literary society, belonged to the debate team, and won a $15 prize in a speech contest.

Like the other college boys, he wore his dark hair parted near the middle and plastered down in the approved style. He was lean, rugged, and popular with the girls at the dances that he helped to organize.

Charlie's favorite professor was Philip Green Wright, a man who was interested in almost everything—English, economics, mathematics, astronomy, poetry, music, art, civil engineering. He was a great teacher because he shared his ideas and enthusiasm with his students.

Fortunately, Professor Wright saw that Charlie had unusual writing ability. He invited Charlie and two other students to come to his house on Sundays to read and discuss their own writing, and to read aloud from works by their favorite authors. They called themselves The Poor Writers Club.

Any time Charlie had a subject that puzzled him, he went to the professor. Soon he found that Wright was as much concerned with improving the life of the common man as he was, and

Charles Sandburg
Class of 1902

together they discussed labor unions, socialism, and communism. They also talked about Abraham Lincoln, in whom the professor was greatly interested.

Charlie promised himself that someday he would learn much more about the Civil War President from Illinois.

Most important, Professor Wright often said to Charlie, "You have a real talent for writing. You must use it more often—write something every day."

In his fourth year of college, Charlie's brother Mart asked, "Well, Charlie, you've tried just about everything now. What are you going to do after you graduate?"

Charlie laughed and then became thoughtful. "I'll be either a writer or a bum," he said.

Mart grinned. "You know, Charlie, I almost believe you."

Mart was wrong about one thing. He believed that Charlie would graduate from Lombard in June. All the family proudly looked forward to that day.

But to everyone's amazement, spring suddenly beckoned to Charlie. Conservative Galesburg hemmed him in. He needed to get away to think for himself, to listen, and to write.

Without a word of explanation he left Lombard to wander again. Sometimes he sold stereoscopic views; sometimes he was a hobo. For six weeks he had a job as police reporter for the New York *Daily News.*

He worked his way through the East — listening, learning, and writing quantities of poetry and prose. He also jotted down folk songs that he heard hoboes and laborers singing.

Two years later he made his way back to Galesburg and his puzzled family. He was twenty-six years old now, and he no longer looked like a dashing college man.

Charlie was sure now that he wanted to make his living as a creative writer. From the East, he had sent Professor Wright some of his poems. Now he decided to take to his friend the rest of the poems and essays he had written during his two years of wandering.

Philip Wright studied them. They were different from anything he and Charlie had read together. Some were impressions of people Charlie had met—poor and troubled people who learned to live with their troubles as his own parents had. Others were his impressions of nature, especially of the prairie land that he loved so much.

"These are interesting, Charlie," Wright said. "They're different. I'd like to print them."

Charlie could hardly believe his ears. "Print them? How?"

"Oh, I have a hand press down in the basement. I can put them into a pamphlet with a paper cover. You'll have to think up a title."

And so, in 1904, Charles A. Sandburg had his name printed on his first book. He called it *In Reckless Ecstasy*. It contained 39 pages in a dark brown cover, tied with a red ribbon.

He dedicated it to his mother, "One who has kept a serene soul in a life of stress, wrested beauty from the commonplace, and scattered good without stint or measure."

Carl Sandburg, 1907.

9. A New Life

Charlie received many congratulations from his friends and family. But after the excitement of seeing his words in print died down, he knew he had outgrown Galesburg for good. He packed his few clothes and the notes from his travels. Then he picked up his banjo, and off he went to Chicago.

There he found a job with a small magazine, *Tomorrow*, which soon published some of his poems and editorials. He liked working for *Tomorrow* because it was a liberal magazine that fought for many good causes, but the publisher paid only for his board and room. So he took a different job with a magazine called *The Lyceumite.*

The Lyceum was an association that for many years had provided lectures, concerts, and other entertainment for towns all over the country. Later, other groups were also formed for the same purpose. *The Lyceumite* served all of them.

"Your job will be to set the ads and write short biographies of performers," the manager told Charlie. "Townspeople read our magazine to decide whom they want to see or hear."

Charlie soon learned that he liked writing about the lives of people. He even billed himself as a lecturer about the poet, Walt Whitman. Charlie greatly admired Whitman's free form of verse. He especially liked his poems about the common man, nature, the Civil War, and Abraham Lincoln. He knew that small-town audiences were not very much interested in Whitman, but after *The Lyceumite* was sold and he lost his job, he lectured whenever he could. He earned a few dollars and learned a great deal about facing people from the platform.

As Charlie traveled about he continued to write poetry. Sometimes the things he wrote had the sound and rhythm of some of Whitman's poetry that he had been reading.

One day that winter, he met Winfield Gaylord who was organizer for the Social-Democratic Party in Wisconsin. They talked about one of Charlie's favorite subjects, the conditions of the poor in the country. The Social-Democratic Party was trying to help them. Gaylord wanted Charlie to be an organizer, too.

"What would I do?" Charlie asked.

"Anything and everything for the party. You'd write pamphlets, give talks, and do your best to find new members. Shall I recommend you?"

"What's the salary?" Charlie asked.

"Whatever you can pick up by passing your hat. That's all. But it's great work."

Charlie agreed. When an offer came in the mail, he accepted. At last he could really work for the underprivileged people of America.

He moved to Milwaukee, Wisconsin, and found that progressive town just what he needed. He

met many intelligent people who wanted the same things that he wanted for the workingman: an eight-hour work day, higher wages, accident insurance, and old-age pensions.

Whenever Charlie talked of these things there was a special ring in his voice, for he thought of his own father, now old and worn. He thought of the fourteen-cent wage he had earned and the twelve-hour days he had worked with no time off. And he remembered the fear his father always had that someday he could no longer work at all.

One day in the office of the party leader, Charlie met a lovely dark-haired young woman.

"Miss Lillian Steichen," the leader said. "This is one of our newest and most active members, Charles Sandburg."

Charlie stammered, "How-do-you-do?" He stayed around until Lillian was ready to leave and then walked to the streetcar with her. From that time on he saw her as often as possible.

He learned that she had graduated from the University of Chicago with high honors and had been teaching for four years. He and Lillian read the same kinds of books. They were both devoted to bettering the lives of the poor. When he showed her his poems, she liked them very much. She invited him to her parents' farm.

Lillian's parents were immigrants from Luxembourg, a very small country between Belgium and Germany. They had given their daughter the nickname of Paus'l. Charlie changed it to Paula.

Paula laughingly accepted the new name. Then she asked, "Why, Carl August Sandburg, do you call yourself Charlie?"

Charlie grinned. "When I was a little boy in Galesburg I wanted an American name — that's why."

Paula tossed her head. "Well, *I'm* going to call you Carl. That sounds strong — like you. It fits you. You should be proud of the fine name that your parents gave you."

Carl smiled. "I've been wanting an excuse to change back for a long time. Now I have the best one in the world."

Paula's parents were not very happy to have their daughter fall in love with a poor poet who did not have a real job. But her older brother, Edward Steichen, a talented photographer, recognized Carl's gift, and Carl, in turn, admired Edward's photography. They became great friends.

Paula and Carl were married on June 15, 1908, when he was thirty years old. They went to Appleton, Wisconsin, and moved into a three-room apartment on the second floor of an old house owned by a member of the party. They paid four dollars a month rent. Paula furnished it with a cheap bed, two chairs, a table, and some orange crates.

From then on, Paula gave up all ambition for herself and devoted her time and thoughts to her husband. She traveled with him whenever she could. Carl consulted her about everything important that he considered doing. She was a great help to him for the rest of his life.

Late in 1909, Carl heard the sad news that his father had fallen from a tree he was pruning and broken his right arm. Before long, the idle life that August Sandburg endured weakened him, and he died of pneumonia in March, 1910.

The news affected Carl deeply. He made up his mind to work harder and moved back to Milwaukee where there would be more opportunities for extra employment.

Besides working for the Social-Democratic Party, Carl wrote advertising copy for a local department store. As he rode on streetcars or sat in waiting rooms, he jotted down ideas for poems, or interesting phrases, or new thoughts.

At night he rewrote and polished his poems. He read them to Paula, who typed them and sent them out to magazines. But no one bought them.

Before long, the writing of advertising copy became too dull for Carl to endure. One day he had a chance to fill in for two weeks as an editorial writer for the Milwaukee *Daily News* while the regular man was on vacation.

He rushed home to ask Paula's advice before accepting.

She saw the gleam in his eyes. "An editorial

writer," she said. "That's what you've always wanted to be, isn't it?"

"Yes," Carl admitted, "ever since I carried papers when I was a boy. I'll be free to say the things that are on my mind." With his wife's blessing, he took the temporary job.

One of his first editorials came straight from his heart. The new Lincoln penny had just been minted, and he was asked to write about it. Carl explained that a rich man finds nothing worth buying for a penny, but that a poor man must watch each one. Then he ended his editorial: "The common, homely face of Honest Abe looks good on the penny, the coin of the common folk from whom he came and to whom he belongs."

He knew that editorial was one of the best things he had ever written.

At about that time, when Paula was away and Carl was lonely, he bought a guitar. He practiced until he could play four chords.

When Paula returned, he played and sang many of the songs he had learned during his travels.

"You'll never find these songs in books, Paula," he told her.

"No," she answered, "but they should be."

When the two weeks were over, Carl took short-time jobs on one newspaper after another. At night he campaigned for the Social-Democratic candidate for mayor. When his man won the election, Carl became his private secretary.

He had no idea what was expected of him, but he soon learned. He had to talk to hundreds of men who had helped in the election and who wanted the mayor to give them jobs or special

Carl and Paula Sandburg, middle, with some of their friends in Milwaukee

favors. Many times, Carl thought of Abraham Lincoln and the troubles he must have had with men like these.

He endured the work for a few months and then went back to the newspaper life that he liked so much, taking a job first as editor for the Social Democratic *Herald* and then as labor reporter for the Milwaukee *Leader.*

New responsibilities had already come to Carl in 1911 when his first daughter, Margaret, was born. He needed more money than he could earn at the *Leader.*

Soon, a newspaper strike hit Chicago. The only paper still being printed there was the Chicago *Daily Socialist.* At once it changed its name to the Chicago *World,* and its small circulation jumped to 600,000.

Carl got a call to hurry to Chicago. This was his great chance, he thought, and Paula agreed. In Chicago they found a small apartment in an old gray house on North Hermitage Street.

Carl went happily to work, but in two weeks the strike was over and the other Chicago papers started printing again. The circulation of the *World* shrank to its former size, and he was soon out of a job.

For the first time in his life, Carl really understood how his father had felt during the hard times. A family man with no job, he went from paper to paper, only to be turned down. In despair he answered every kind of advertisement. He tried to get a job addressing envelopes.

He could not even borrow any money, for in Chicago he had no friends.

One morning he walked into a basement office in a poor west-side neighborhood. There, stacked on a desk, were copies of a very small newspaper, the *Day Book*. He thumbed through the twelve pages of cheap newsprint. No advertising! What kind of a paper was this? He looked at a story and liked what he read — outspoken statements about events in the city.

A man glanced up wearily.

"You looking for a paper or a job?" he asked.

Carl grinned. "A job," he said.

Quickly he told the man of the jobs he had

held and how he happened to be out of work in Chicago. Then he learned about the *Day Book*. It was an experiment. In it a writer could say what he wanted to without fear of offending an advertiser because there were no ads.

"We need another reporter—$25 a week, if you want the job," the man said.

Carl raced home to tell Paula. They danced around their bare apartment in excitement.

The next morning he began hunting for news — the kind that he liked to write about. He wrote

Horse-drawn wagons and early automobiles shared the streets of Carl Sandburg's Chicago in 1911.

of accidents in factories. He searched out facts that no other paper would print.

As he waited to interview people, he jotted down poems on little scraps of paper and stuffed them into his pockets. These were better than his earlier efforts, he knew. He was writing about the Chicago that he cared so much about.

He read to Paula one evening:

> The fog comes
> on little cat feet.
>
> It sits looking
> over harbor and city
> on silent haunches
> and then moves on.

"That's the way it came today," he told her. "I wrote that while I waited in the courthouse to see the juvenile court judge."

"It's very good, Carl," Paula said. "Someday Margaret will like it. And other children will like it, too."

They had no idea how many thousands of school children would read and memorize those words.

Some time later, Paula gathered together nine of Carl's Chicago poems. She sent them to Harriet Monroe, who was editor of a new magazine called *Poetry*.

At first Miss Monroe was shocked by what she read. No one had ever sent her poetry about the brutal stockyards and other ugly parts of the city. She started again, saying the words aloud:

> Hog Butcher for the World,
> Tool Maker, Stacker of Wheat,
> Player with Railroads and the
> Nation's Freight Handlers;
> Stormy, husky, brawling,
> City of the Big Shoulders.

Fascinated, Miss Monroe read all nine poems. This man, Carl Sandburg, was writing about Chicago as though it were a husky, brawling person. The lines did not rhyme but they had a stormy, protesting sound that appealed to her. They pictured Chicago as it really was—brutal, sad, lonely, but sometimes gentle.

She decided to publish them on the first nine pages of the March, 1914, issue of her magazine, and she sent the author a check for $100. Later that year her recommendation helped Carl receive the Helen Haire Levinson Prize of $200 for having written the best poems of the year.

The Sandburgs could hardly believe their good fortune. They were still very poor.

"Now we can move to a larger house where you can have a room of your own for your writing," Paula exclaimed. "I've seen one out in Maywood that I like."

"You make the arrangements," Carl said. "We've lived in crowded rooms long enough."

The house into which they moved in 1915 made a great difference in their lives. But most important to both of them was the knowledge that Carl, at age thirty-six, had at last received the recognition which he deserved.

10. Recognition and Rewards

Not everyone liked Carl's poetry. Some said it was not poetry at all, because it did not rhyme. A few of the lines were only a word or two, and others were more than 100 words long. Some words were slang, and some of the ideas were rough and tough.

But many who read the poetry thought it very original and said that the author had great promise.

One person who believed in Carl was Miss Monroe's assistant, Alice Corbin. The next year when she went to New York, she took a packet of his poems to Alfred Harcourt, a salesman for the publishers, Henry Holt and Company.

Mr. Harcourt liked the poems very much, but he had a hard time persuading his employer to publish them. Finally he succeeded, and the book called *Chicago Poems* appeared in the spring of 1916. It contained nearly 100 poems.

Carl had dedicated it "To My Wife and Pal, Lillian Steichen Sandburg." When he put his arm around her and placed the first copy in her hand he said, "Without your help and encouragement it might never have been published."

Before long everyone seemed to be talking about the reporter-poet. Many other writers in Chicago wanted to know him, so they arranged to meet in one of the restaurants where Carl often lunched.

They were amazed when they saw him. He did not look or act like a Chicago reporter or even a poet. He looked like a farmer or a factory worker.

He ambled into the restaurant, muffled in a

long scarf and wearing an ugly old black rain cap with a broken visor.

He smiled pleasantly at everyone and unwound his long muffler. His pockets bulged and overflowed with pencils, scraps of paper, and old yellowed newspaper clippings. His hair looked as though he had cut it himself. His shirt collar was frayed, and his suit was rumpled and baggy.

Without looking at a menu he ordered, "Coffee and ham-on-rye." He did not notice the interesting food on other plates, for a sandwich filled his stomach when he was hungry. Besides, ham-on-rye was cheap.

When they finished eating, a friend asked Carl to read some of his poems.

He rummaged through his pockets until he found the one he had been working on. It had been written in pencil on a scrap of yellow paper.

As soon as he began to read, the group around the table forgot about Carl's hair, his rumpled suit, his frayed collar. They saw his strong, workingman hands holding the yellow paper, and they heard his deep rich voice read slowly, deliberately, the words he had so carefully written.

His face was stern throughout the reading. He did not try to dramatize the poem.

By the time Carl finished, the men who had smiled at his appearance were greatly impressed. This poet was obviously one of the "common" men of whom he wrote. He spoke for them.

When another daughter, Janet, was born in 1916, the Sandburgs were glad they had moved to the larger house. But unfortunately, after the United States entered World War I in 1917, the owner of the *Day Book* decided to close down the newspaper, and Carl was out of a job once again.

At thirty-nine, he had to find a new source of income. Quickly he sorted through his many poems and selected a large group about his boyhood and some of the people and places he had seen during his hobo days. He called the collection *Cornhuskers* and dedicated it to his little daughters, Janet and Margaret.

First in the collection was one of the longest

poems that Carl ever wrote. Into it he had put his great love of the prairie. It begins:

> I was born on the prairie and the
>   milk of its wheat, the red of
>   its clover, the eyes of its women,
>   gave me a song and a slogan.

Cornhuskers was published in 1918. For it, he shared the Poetry Society of America Prize that year with Margaret Widdemer.

But books of poetry could not support a growing family. Meanwhile, a friend, realizing this, had gone to the Managing Editor of the Chicago *Daily News*, Henry J. Smith.

"I know a man you should hire," he said. "You've heard of him — Carl Sandburg. He's not only a poet but also a fine reporter."

Mr. Smith smiled. He believed that the men who worked on the *Daily News* should be more than just reporters; he liked to encourage talented people.

"We need a good poet," he said. "I'll see him."

Shortly afterward, Carl talked with Mr. Smith and in ten minutes was offered a job.

Carl could hardly believe his good fortune. He remembered when he had carried the *Daily News* in Galesburg and had read every word of it at night.

"It's a fine, liberal paper," he told Paula joyfully. "And I'll get $50 a week — twice as much as I made on the *Day Book*."

And so Carl Sandburg began his years with the Chicago *Daily News*. He loved his work, for he was allowed to write exactly what he wished.

On one assignment, he roamed the Negro district and wrote a series of articles about much that he saw and heard. He told about the over-crowded slums behind the smelly stockyards, where the Negroes lived. He told of the high rents they were forced to pay. He warned that riots would soon erupt if the Negroes did not get fair treatment.

One day at a Lake Michigan beach, while Carl was still writing the series, a Negro boy ventured into a "white only" area. Some white boys threw stones at him and pushed him off a raft. The boy drowned.

Negroes tried to get a policeman nearby to arrest the white boys. When he refused, fights broke out. From there, riots spread all over Chicago.

Carl rushed his stories to the *Daily News*.

The series on the riots was also sent to Alfred Harcourt, who liked it very much. In 1919, the new publishing company he had helped to form, Harcourt, Brace and Howe, printed the articles in a 50¢ pamphlet called *The Chicago Race Riots*.

Carl's interest in the Negroes and in Abraham Lincoln were inseparable. He wrote about both in his poetry. And he cared deeply about both of them all his life.

The managing editor of the paper, Mr. Smith, understood how important it was for Carl to have uninterrupted time to write his poetry, so he appointed him movie editor.

"You can see all the movies on two days and nights each week," he said. "You can have the rest of the week for your own writing."

Carl and Paula Sandburg at Elmhurst, 1923

Carl was very grateful. He worked at the office until long after midnight on those two days, getting his reviews ready for the week. Then he took the train out to the suburb where he lived.

But it was hard to work in the noise of the growing suburb. And the house did not seem so large now that the baby, Helga, was born.

Besides, he needed more room for himself. For years he had been collecting clippings and books, many of them about Abraham Lincoln. Overflowing boxes were stored in every corner.

So he moved his family farther from the city to the village of Elmhurst. The white frame house at 331 South York Street was over seventy years old. It had once been a little schoolhouse; later one room after another had been added haphazardly.

Life at Elmhurst was happy and relaxed. Carl called Paula "My Pal," and she called him "My Buddy."

The house was full of pets, and the children raced in and out. They squealed whenever they saw their beloved Uncle Edward come up the walk with his camera. He played with them, and they posed for many pictures.

But the best time of the day always came just after dinner.

"Is anyone for a story?" Carl asked.

"Oh, *yes*," the girls shouted.

"Well, what shall it be this time?"

"About Bimbo the Snip," Margaret cried.

"I want Shush Shush!" Janet wailed.

"Bimbo the Snip," Margaret insisted. "It's funnier. Anyway, I asked first."

"Sh-h-h," their mother cautioned. "You chose yesterday, Margaret. It's Janet's turn."

"Shush Shush, Daddy," Janet said firmly.

"All right, Skabootch," Carl agreed, using his pet name for her.

No one moved while he began to read.

"Shush Shush was a big buff banty hen. She lived in a coop. Sometimes she marched out of the coop and went away and laid eggs. But always she came back to the coop.

"And whenever she went to the front door and laid an egg in the door-bell, she rang the bell once for one egg, twice for two eggs, and a dozen rings for a dozen eggs."

The girls giggled. "Go on, Daddy," Janet whispered.

Carl read to the end of the story. "Tomorrow we'll have Bimbo the Snip," he said.

Margaret sighed. "Please, Daddy, will you put the stories in a book so I can read them? There aren't any half as good in the library."

Carl smiled. "I'll do that, Spink," he promised.

Carl did gather them into a book called *Rootabaga Stories* and dedicated them to Spink and Skabootch. His friend Alfred Harcourt published them in 1922, and later another volume, *Rootabaga Pigeons*. They sold so well that Carl was able to borrow $600 from Mr. Harcourt to help pay for the vacant lot next door where a house was to be built. He wanted to make a beautiful garden there and keep his privacy.

Up the steep stairway at the back of the house was Carl's own study, where he often worked throughout the night in perfect solitude. It was a plain room, furnished with straw matting for a rug, some old desks and tables, and pine shelves all around. On the shelves were his books about Lincoln and other books of old folk songs. The rest of the room was crowded with war-surplus metal record files loaded with his clippings.

"Pretty soon I may have to store some of

these," he would say to Paula as he added more to his collection.

In that room at Elmhurst, Carl polished and prepared for publication two more books of poetry, *Smoke and Steel* and *Slabs of the Sunburnt West*. The first, he dedicated to his brother-in-law, Edward Steichen, for whom he had great respect and affection. The second he dedicated to his baby daughter, Helga.

The poems in both books repeated many of the subjects of his earlier books: America, the

Carl could always find time for a secret or some fun with Helga (left) and Margaret.

common man, nature, the city. The forms of his poems were the same as they had always been.

Besides all his other work, Carl lectured and read his poems for a Lyceum bureau. Billed as "The Well-known Poet," he had many engagements. In small towns in Illinois, Abraham Lincoln's home state, he talked with people who had known Lincoln or had heard stories about him. Since he was planning to write a series of three books about the famous man, he needed all the material he could get. He added many stories to his collection.

He also continued to listen for new folk songs among work gangs and harvest hands.

One January evening in 1921, Carl was to read his poetry for the students at Cornell College in Mount Vernon, Iowa. It was his first appearance before a college audience. For some reason, he decided to take his guitar with him.

After he had read his poetry he said, "At home I play my guitar in the evenings. Since I'm not at home, I'm going to play it now. If you don't want to stay, it's all right with me."

CARL SANDBURG

Lecture - recital: readings
from his books, "Chicago
Poems," "Cornhuskers,"
"Smoke and Steel."

Bookings of Mr. Sandburg for platform
engagements, address:

Mitchell Dawson,
First National Bank Bldg., Chicago

Then he tuned up his guitar, strummed his four chords, and began to sing some of the folk songs that he liked best. The astonished students listened to "Jesse James."

It was on a Wednesday night,
　　the moon was shining bright,
They robbed the Glendale train.
And the people they did say,
　　for many miles away,
'Twas the outlaws Frank
　　and Jesse James.

Then they heard songs of the harvest fields and songs of the rivers and steamboats. They applauded for more and more.

From that day on, Carl always ended his readings with his folk songs. His popularity as a performer grew enormously.

11. Abraham Lincoln

Newspaperman, poet, writer of stories for children, platform artist, collector of American folk songs — Carl Sandburg was many things to many people.

But to his family and to himself at this time, he was becoming more and more the collector of Lincoln material.

When he was called to New York by Mr. Harcourt to talk about another book for children, he suggested writing about Lincoln.

Mr. Harcourt agreed to let him try.

When Carl got home he told Paula and the two older girls, who thought it a fine idea. But first, he reminded them, he would have to sort and file his many clippings and notes.

Carl enjoyed his sorting immensely, chuckling over some of the old clippings as he read them. Paula often helped him and shared his pleasure.

Sometimes, when Carl found an unusual item, he thought of sharing it with the girls. But he realized that probably they would not find it very interesting.

How could they understand or care as much about Lincoln as he did? They had never been hungry; they had never lived far from the big city.

Only he, of all the family, could really understand. He had lived with a father who could not write his own name; Lincoln's mother could not write hers. Both he and Lincoln had known real poverty and hard labor. Both had known the smell of the prairie and the feel of the earth under their bare feet. Both had longed for an education and had devoured all the books they could get. Both had had periods of deep despair but had kept their sense of humor.

Far into the night Carl searched for facts and wrote and rewrote his pages. Sometimes it was dawn before he stopped.

Meanwhile, he had to earn a living for his family of five. Two days a week he worked on his movie reviews for the *Daily News*. At least 30 times each year he went off somewhere to lecture, read his poetry, and sing folk songs for an ever more demanding public.

Then back in his study at Elmhurst, he would catalogue any new material he had found and take up his writing again.

Before long he knew that what he was writing was not a book for children. His stack of pages grew taller and taller. If he left out any of the material, he seemed to spoil the story.

At last, after more than two years, the book was finished. He called it *Abraham Lincoln: The Prairie Years*. Instead of the 400 pages he had promised, he had more than 1,100.

But Alfred Harcourt did not complain. In fact he persuaded the editor of the magazine, the *Pictorial Review*, to publish part of it as a serial.

He saw to it that Carl received $30,000 for the magazine rights.

"Thirty thousand!" Paula exclaimed when he told her. "Just think—only six years ago we borrowed six hundred dollars to buy the lot next door and keep our privacy."

Now their privacy was even more important. Elmhurst was growing into a busy, noisy suburb. And many people, often strangers, now came to see Carl. Although he always liked to talk to them, he needed more time for his work.

They bought a summer house on the east side of Lake Michigan at Tower Hill near Harbert. Although they did not have the privacy they had hoped for, they enjoyed swimming in the cool water. Edward Steichen, by now a famous photographer, came often and romped with them on the white sand dunes.

In February, 1926, on the 117th anniversary of Lincoln's birthday, Sandburg's huge work was published in two volumes. He dedicated it to his mother, who died before the year ended, knowing that her eldest son had become a famous man.

Carl Sandburg and Edward Steichen were friends
as well as brothers-in-law.

The story starts with Lincoln's ancestors in
1776, and ends just as the new president leaves
for Washington and his inauguration.

Carl had not tried to explain Lincoln. By putting
together all the facts he could find, he showed
the readers a real human being with problems
and faults, with courage and humility. He showed
them the America of Lincoln's time and the
simple prairie country in which he lived.

Reviewers from all over the world gave Carl the highest praise for his great work. They called it a classic.

All the praise did not change Carl. He kept his job with the *Daily News* for six more years, but instead of writing movie reviews, he wrote a column called "From the Notebook of Carl Sandburg." He could write about anything he wanted to. His name drew readers by the thousands. He also continued his lectures and singing.

Financial security made some difference, for now Carl had time to arrange the folk songs that he had been collecting for 30 years. He wrote something of their history and where he found them. He hired composers to write the music.

The American Songbag was published the next year. It gave Carl almost as much pleasure as his Lincoln biography had. Then the first 26 chapters of *The Prairie Years* were published as a book for young people, called *Abe Lincoln Grows Up*. Another collection of poetry, *Good Morning, America*, also came out.

A moment of solitude at Lake Michigan

Now the family looked for a different home on the lake, one that would give them real privacy. In time they found just the place they wanted, surrounded by five acres of land. They planned to convert the summer house into a year-round home.

The girls were delighted. Living at the lake was much better than living in Elmhurst, they thought. Janet and Helga did not mind the idea of walking a mile to the highway, even in winter, to catch the bus that would take them to school in Three Oaks.

One day Helga announced, "I want to be a farmer. I want a cow!"

"Not a cow!" Carl exclaimed. "How about goats? They would be easier to handle and could eat off some of the underbrush."

Everyone laughed.

"Remember Heidi and how she drank bowls of goat milk?" Margaret said.

Carl surrounded by his family—Paula and, left to right, Helga, Janet, Margaret

"We could have goats' milk and cheese and butter," Paula added. "We could even buy those adjoining two acres. But we should have beautiful goats — not just ordinary ones."

Carl tilted back in his chair and smiled. "Chikaming Goat Farm. How's that for an old Indian name?"

The barn and the goats came much later. Paula was kept busy supervising the work on the house. She had the walls insulated and the porch screens changed to glass.

Most important was Carl's study in the attic. It opened onto a sun deck where he could set up his typewriter during clear, warm days. Paula furnished the big study with a wood-burning stove, a cot, and the usual assortment of old desks and tables. She had the walls lined with unfinished shelves for the hundreds of books that must be moved from Elmhurst. Carl brought in a wooden crate that was just the right height for his typewriter.

In 1928 the house was ready. When they moved all the cartons of unused Lincoln material into

Carl and "tenant" at Chikaming Goat Farm

the study, Paula asked, "What in the world are you going to do with all this?"

Carl looked happily around his room, filled with all the things that he loved.

"It's been six years since *The Prairie Years* was published," he said. "Maybe I should write an epilogue. I'm fifty-four years old. That seems about the right age to start it."

12. Two Great Lives End

The "epilogue" was not so simple as it sounded. When Carl worked over the notes he had on Lincoln's years in Washington, he discovered many gaps.

"It's going to be a bigger job than I imagined," he told Paula. "I want to know everything about Lincoln and put it all down in my book."

Paula laughed. "Your book! You'll never get all that into one volume," she said.

Before long, Carl knew that she was right. He looked everywhere for facts about everyone who worked with Lincoln during his years as president. Sometimes he even went into Chicago and sat cross-legged on the sidewalk beside outdoor bookstands where he thumbed through old magazines.

Few of his fans recognized him there. But old friends smiled as they passed the familiar raw-boned figure wearing a green eyeshade over his ragged white hair.

In spite of Carl's successes, he had the uneasy feeling that he must have more security for his wife and children. The great depression of the thirties was on, and men were selling apples on the streets to keep alive. He remembered the hard times of 1893 and what they had done to his father.

And so he continued his lectures. He also wrote more poetry. In 1936 he published another volume, *The People, Yes*.

The book was a collection of sketches and folklore about hardworking Americans. Its theme —their triumph over hardship—gave hope to many people during the depression.

At the very end of the book, Carl wrote:

In the darkness with a great bundle
     of grief the people march,
In the night, and overhead a shovel
     of stars for keeps, the people march:
     "Where to? what next?"

In general the book was well received. But some of Carl's critics said that he had not grown as a poet and had nothing new to say. He was still the spokesman for the people and had said so many times before.

The hours in the attic room grew longer and longer. Far into the night he worked. In the mornings he slept. When he wakened he found breakfast on a tray outside his door, with a thermos of hot coffee to help him start another day. Through beautiful spring, summer, and fall days he worked.

The girls, all still at home, helped when they could. Sometimes a secretary sorted and copied for him and helped with letters.

When Paula was not needed, she spent her time caring for the goats. She and the girls took them to fairs and often came home with blue ribbons. They all loved the farm and spent as much time out of doors as possible.

Paula was now white-haired, too, but her face was still serene and her cheeks pink. She was happy knowing that Carl was doing what he wanted most to do.

As Carl neared his sixtieth birthday the book was becoming huge. Sometimes his nerves

Sometimes Carl managed to steal a few moments to help Helga and Paula with the goats.

were tense. The sound of laughter outside on a beautiful day would annoy him.

"A little less noise down there," he would call from above. "How can I work?"

Then the girls would tiptoe quietly away.

They worried about him but could say nothing. They understood that their father was going through the terrible tragedy of the Civil War years with Abraham Lincoln.

Toward the last, Carl began to have many doubts about his work. It was too long. No one would read it, he said, but he had to finish.

At last the day came when he wrote of Lincoln's assassination and death. Carl had lived with him for so long that he seemed to be watching the death of his dearest friend. He wrote at the end:

"And then night came with great quiet.
And there was rest.
The prairie years, the war years, were over."

Tears began to flow down Carl's cheeks. For two hours he could not stop them. His great work was over. His dear friend of many years was gone — and he was exhausted.

Fortunately for Carl, the work was not entirely over as he had thought. The halt would have been too sudden for him. For five months he worked in the home of a publisher's assistant, and together they got the 3,400 typed sheets ready for the printer. Carl wrote captions for the pictures and read the printer's proofs.

By the time he got back to the farm, the emotional experience of finishing the book was in the past. He was his usual happy self.

The first 29,000 sets of *Abraham Lincoln: The War Years* were published in 1939. Although the four volumes cost twenty dollars, they were sold at once. Praise was heaped upon the monumental work. It was called one of the great biographies of the time.

The author was awarded the Pulitzer Prize for having written the best work of history that year. He received many other honors and awards.

Carl Sandburg was never again to have the solitude that he once had craved. Though he

Carl, now world famous as an author and poet, posed for Jo Davidson, a well-known sculptor.

continued to write some minor works, among them an historical novel, *Remembrance Rock*, he greatly slowed his pace. He began to enjoy being a public figure.

He joined many organizations and attended meetings when he could. He even went back to Galesburg in 1940 for a reunion of Company C. He was given many honorary degrees by outstanding universities, including Harvard and Yale. Six high schools and five elementary schools were named for him.

The Republican Party wanted him to run for president. The Democratic Party wanted him for the House of Representatives. He refused both requests.

At home, life became more normal. Although Helga was now married, with a home of her own, Margaret and Janet helped keep the family spirits high. Carl admired Paula's herd of prize goats. They took walks together and visited with neighbors. He played his guitar and sang again.

But as he neared his seventieth birthday, he had to admit that the damp air from the lake was not good for him. Besides, the herd of goats was growing too large for seven acres. He loved the lake and the sand dunes, but he knew he must leave.

"Where shall we go?" Paula asked.

Carl smiled. "I picked the dunes," he said. "Now you pick the next place."

In North Carolina, near Flat Rock, Paula found an 1839 white clapboard farm house on 241 acres. The climate was mild and the house with its many windows was warmed by sunlight. The farm had rolling foothills, huge pines and oaks, and grass-land for the 72 goats. It was called "Connemara."

Paula had bookcases built to reach the fifteen-foot ceilings in nearly every room.

When Carl came into the sunny, spacious house and saw the many bookshelves filled with books, he said, "When I was a boy, my dear mother bought me a book. I promised myself then that someday I would have many books with shelves to put them on. But I never imagined anything like this."

Carl at work in the study at Connemara

In 1945, when he was settled in his new home, Carl was at peace. He again received the Pulitzer Prize, this time for his *Complete Poems*, published in 1950.

He decided that the time had come to write about his own life.

He set to work putting onto paper a quiet, complete, often humorous story of his life in Galesburg from the time he was born until he was twenty years old. He included his family, the town, and his thoughts about them and himself.

In the book, the reader can find the beginning of all that Carl Sandburg was going to become.

Always the Young Strangers was published in 1953, when Carl was seventy-five years old. One fine writer called it "the best autobiography ever written by an American." It was a remarkable achievement for a man of any age.

Later, a short version called *Prairie Town Boy* was published for young readers. Carl also wrote an introduction for Edward Steichen's great collection of photographs, *Family of Man*, published in 1955.

Carl was a friend both of the young and the famous. Above, with Roddy Knoop and, below, with President John F. Kennedy

Carl continued to work, for he did not know how to stop. He had worked all his life. He read a great deal, marking passages that he liked with long, thin strips of newspaper. He wrote a little prose or poetry every day, wearing his old green eyeshade as usual.

Sometimes he talked of writing a sequel to his autobiography. He had other plans for more books. But he was growing older; his years of writing were coming to an end.

In June, 1967, when he was 89, Carl Sandburg had his first heart attack. A few weeks later he had another. On July 22, Paula found that he had died peacefully in his sleep.

Sadly but proudly she repeated the words that had been said of Abraham Lincoln: "Now he belongs to the ages."

Home at Connemara Farms

Books for Young People by Carl Sandburg

ROOTABAGA STORIES
New York: Harcourt, Brace, 1922.

ROOTABAGA PIGEONS
New York: Harcourt, Brace, 1923.

ABE LINCOLN GROWS UP
New York: Harcourt, Brace, 1928.
(From *Abraham Lincoln: The Prairie Years*—
first twenty-six chapters.)

ROOTABAGA COUNTRY
New York: Harcourt, Brace, 1929. (Selections.)

EARLY MOON
New York: Harcourt, Brace, 1930. (Selection of poems.)

POTATO FACE
New York: Harcourt, Brace, 1930.

ROOTABAGA STORIES
New York: Harcourt, Brace, 1936. (Complete.)

PRAIRIE TOWN BOY
New York: Harcourt, Brace, 1955.
(From *Always the Young Strangers.)*

WIND SONG
New York: Harcourt, Brace, 1960. (Selection of poems.)

Index

144

Date Due

AP 16 '73					
NO 28 '73					
MR 25 74					
AP 2 '74					
AP 22 74					
APR 11 '79					
MAY 8 '79					
MAY 11 '85					